T0167040

Today,
Tomorrow,
Yesterday

Today, Tomorrow, Yesterday

A Poetry Collection

NICKADIA DANIELS

Order this book online at www.trafford.com
or email orders@trafford.com

Most Trafford titles are also available at major online book retailers.

Printed in the United States of America.

ISBN: 978-1-4269-6103-8 (sc)
ISBN: 978-1-4269-6116-8 (e)

Trafford rev. 12/14/2012

 www.trafford.com

North America & International
toll-free: 1 888 232 4444 (USA & Canada)
phone: 250 383 6864 ♦ fax: 812 355 4082

This book of poetry is dedicated to the memory of my mother, Willie Dell Williams, a poet herself; but never published.

TABLE OF CONTENTS

DEDICATIONS

FAMILY

HERITAGE

RELATIONSHIPS

INSPIRATIONS

SOCIETY/SOCIAL CONCERNS

SELF-ESTEEM

RANDOM THOUGHTS

DEDICATIONS

Willie D

June 30, 1905, she came to life.
April 8, 1984, she succumbed to death.
The years between she became
Willie D by name.

Who was she?
First, a child raised up alone.
No sister or brother
just she alone.

Parents to care for her—
Oh, that was sure
and they shed their love
for her year by year.

Now, grown up
she became a mother
giving birth at first
to one lone daughter.

As the years passed,
she mothered others
fourteen the total
four preceded her in death.

Some years between
the first four or five
she sat by her own mother's side
as Christ came to call her home.

Just as the last of her children were born
a daughter made her a new grandmother.

The years passed on and
she made it through her fears.
Praying each day,
"Lord help my tears."

A mother and now a grandmother too,
Willie D also took charge of that task.
She cooked, she cleaned,
she made her house a home.

People came from miles
to eat from her table.

She gave of her life, she gave of her love
Willie D, she gave of whatever
she was.

Fortune and fame she never proclaimed.
Yet Willie D was of the talented sort.

A poet, never printed.
A seamstress never discovered.

Willie D, it was said,
could do anything.

Just as everyone else,
Willie D was sent by God
to perform a special task
that of being our blessed mother.

While You're yet Alive

While you're yet alive,
I will do all that I can do.
I will send you flowers
and run your errands.
I will call you on the phone
and we can talk for hours.
There isn't anything that
I will not do for you,
while you're yet alive.

I don't know what will happen
when you are gone;
but I know that nothing I do
will bring you back
to this particular home.
That is why, on this day,
I attest that I will do
all I can for you,
while you're yet alive.

Why should I give you flowers
when you're gone?
You won't know they are there.
You can't hold them in your arms
and smell the sweet fragrance
of their bouquet.
That is the reason why
I will send you flowers
while you're yet alive.

I will cry with you
over the pain and sorrow
for I know the crying
I do after you're gone
will not help the suffering
you've gone through today;
that is why I will honor you
while you're yet alive.

Yes, I will do all I can for you
for I know not what
tomorrow will bring
after you're gone;
but I know that it will not
return you to this particular shore
for me to wait for you to leave,
then call upon Jesus
to let you know
that I meant to do all that I
could for you
while you were yet alive.

A Young Man Dies

A young man dies.
His mother cries.
A father never knows
the loss.

In the church
a casket closed
opens to a view—
the last.

A family cries
from the horror.
The boy who died was
a scholar.

A restaurant close by
people laughing
then makes trouble
for the owner.
The bullet that
pierced the body
was not from a foe.

He died at the
hands of his family—
the ones who
loved him most.

Forever

People say that nothing lasts forever;
but what is forever?
Is it the eternity that some people never see—
the yesterday that's faded in years gone by?
Is it the mystery that man searches for—
the inner depths of our souls?

Forever may be today,
        or it may be tomorrow.
It may be this minute—
        or the next.

Forever could be the time we have already shared
        or it may be the time we have yet to share.

Forever may be the memories we keep
        bottled in our minds;
        the smiles that pass our lips.

Forever may be the tears we shed
        in joy or sorrow.
        It may be the songs of the little sparrow.

Forever may be in a hug or a kiss
        or forever may be the times we wish to last.
        It may be the twinkle of an eye
        or the kindness of a stranger.

Forever may be the life God gave us
     when we were born.
     It may be the blanket that keeps us warm.
     It may be the promise of no harm.

F   o   r   e   v   e   r
I cannot explain, but I hope our friendship is forever—
whatever forever brings.

(Dedicated and written to a very dear friend, who means so very much
to me.)

Grandmother

Dear Grandmother:

Although you do not know me, I feel compelled to write and wish you a very happy 90th birthday.

When I told your namesake, that I wanted to send you a birthday card, I knew that it would not be just some card I picked up in the supermarket or even from a Hallmark® store. I knew that I wanted to write something elegant; but then I got a case of writer's block. I thought who am I and what can I say to an older woman whom I don't know and have never met. Then I thought: 'If this were my grandmother, what would I say to her for her 90th birthday?' Since I never knew my maternal grandmother and only knew my paternal grandmother for a short while, I decided that I think I would want to say this to them had they lived to be ninety-years young. I hope you do not mind if I call you grandmother. Here goes . . .

Grandmother,

God has given you a very special time and purpose in this life. He has given you life abundant. Perhaps as a child you never dreamed of seeing fifty; but now you are ninety. What a blessing!! You must be very proud. You have seen so much and done so much. Your life is filled with many memories, no matter what they hold. I'm sure that there have been things in your life that you would rather not remember. But there are also, memories that you have enjoyed and want to share. Whatever the memories or things you've faced, God has brought you through them all. You have raised your family and watched over each generation as they have made their way.

Through the years, you've watched so much history unfold. You have so much to offer to us the younger generations who must carry on for many years to come. You have so much wisdom to teach us. We need only to listen and learn from you. Count it all joy that God has given you so many years to share the knowledge you have.

Grandmother, I hope your children, grandchildren, great-grandchildren, and future generations know what they have in you. I hope you know what you have in them. You have a very good legacy to leave your family. Tell them of your past, so they may learn from it and wax strong. I wish my grandparents had lived long enough for me to ask them questions about their life when they were young. I admire those of you who came before me and blazed a trail for me to follow. Some may say that you made mistakes; but who has lived and not made mistakes? We of the younger generations need to learn that you came before us for a reason. As I often tell my youngest son, "God put me here as your parent, because evidently, He felt that I would make a better parent to you than you would to me." I have always looked to the older generations for guidance for that reason. God put you here before us because He felt that you would be better teachers to us than we would be to you.

Grandmother, I hope I have not bored you with lots of words that mean nothing. I don't have a lot of wisdom, just a warm heart. It gives me pleasure to send you this greeting to wish you the very best birthday, and share in your joy of reaching ninety years.

May your children, grandchildren, and great-grandchildren know what a jewel they have in having had you with them this number of years. May you have many, many more.

God bless you and keep you in His care.

Happy 90th Birthday Grandmother

A granddaughter by virtue of our history.

Thank You Mom

For the nine months you carried me.
Thank you, mom.

For all the long nights you stayed with me;
wept for me, prayed for me.
Thank you, mom.

For all the many thing you've done for me;
comforted me, cheered me up when I was blue,
wiped my tears and kissed away my hurts and pains.
Thank you, mom.

For all the years that lie ahead and
the ones that are gone before.
Thank you, mom.

Thank you mom for being you,
for being here when I've needed you,
(and when I didn't).

For all the things you've taught me
and everything you've bought me.
Thank you, mom.

I know it's not been an easy task
to have me and hold me;
but you've never given up.
You're always there when I need you.
So for all of this and things to come,
I thank you mom.

Take Time

Take time to work
it is the price of success.

Take time to think
it is the source of power.

Take time to play
it is the secret of perpetual youth.

Take time to read
it is the fountain of wisdom.

Take time to worship
it is the highway to reverence.

Take time to be friendly
it is the road to happiness.

Take time to laugh
it is the music of the soul.

Take time to dream
it is hitching your wagon to a star.

Take time to live . . .

A Step Between

You've grown up
from a tiny tot
and although you've
not reached the top
you're just a step below
you know
just a step in between.

The years have passed;
but memories last
of the days long gone
which cannot be captured
or thought upon.

When you were young,
mom and dad
held you in their arms,
you were just a step
below the walking
stage you know.

As you grew, with each obstacle
you overcame,
there was always one
more to conquer,
leaving you one more step to go.
Now, as you walk across
the stage,
take time to look back
on the past,
then know as you go forth
you're just one step between
becoming an adult
and striking out on your own.
No matter how much you grow,
you're always just a step
between
life's eternal door.

Though We Quarrel

Though the time gets a little rough
and the going a little tough
and though we sometime quarrel
aren't you glad we never fight.

Let's start a new life,
kiss and make up,
and love each other till
the end of time.

(Dedicated to the memory of Dr. Richard Galton)

FAMILY

Quilt Pieces

(Piecing it all together)

Your dad and my dad don't have the same name
yet you and I are sisters just the same.
You're my brother because
your dad and my dad are one and the same.
Yet my mother and your mother are very different
in the way they walk
and the way they talk;
but us two,
we're family just the same.

My uncle is your daddy,
my sister is your mother;
that makes you my niece and
my cousin.

Double kin we are
and no one was ever ashamed.

Daddy died and left us
a brother here,
a sister there.
Mother left behind
children bound
by the blood of her veins
and yet we are now strangers,
or so it seems.

My children don't know your children.
Your children don't know mine.
Yet we're all here trying to
knit, weave the pieces together,
quilting—making the pieces fit.
We're related, or are we?

My dad and your dad are one.
Your mom and my mom are the same.
We're family, or are we?
Trying to join the quilt;
but the seams don't seem to fit.
The thread seems to keep breaking,
there's no hope of quilting.
The pieces are not fitting.

A cut here, a tuck there
we're all related
aren't we?

You're my cousin because
my mother is your daddy's baby mama
and daddy is mother's baby daddy,
that makes us related,
or are we?

I don't want no baby's daddy,
won't be no baby's mama,
not if we're not married
for life—
forever.

I won't be your baby's mama.
You won't be my baby's daddy.
We won't leave our children here,
trying to piece the pieces together.

You my brother!
You my sister!
She my sister!
He my brother!
We just here trying to make
sense of the threads our parents left us.
We have the same blood,
yet it's different.

His mother is not my mother.
Yet, he be my brother.
My daddy is not her daddy.
Yet, we are sisters.

It's not the same for us,
you and me.
we share
and yet we're not altogether whole
because
your daddy was my mother's
baby daddy.

When You Were Mother

Used to be when you were mother,
you chastised me.
Then you became mom
and wanted to be my friend.

Used to be when you were mother,
there were rules.
Now that you are mom,
there are time outs.

Used to be when you were mother,
you chose my clothes.
Now that you are mom,
I wear what I choose.

Used to be when you were mother,
I had respect for my elders.
Now that you are mom,
I call your friends by their first name.

Used to be when you were mother
I chose my friends carefully.
Now that you are mom
my friends can be anyone.

Used to be when you were mother
my life was not stressed
because my choices were never guessed.
Now that you are mom
the decisions I make are most likely mistakes.

What is a Man?

My dear son, it is today that the world will begin to look
upon you as a man, for today you turn twenty-one.

What, My Son, Is A Man?

A man is the male species of the human race
a man is responsible for his actions,
a man realizes there are choices and that
for each choice he makes there are consequences.
A man accepts the things he cannot change,
changes the things he can,
and has the insight to know what
he can and cannot change.
A man has integrity,
is a man of his word,
and will let nothing stand in the way
of his carrying out his word.
A man has pride about himself.

There are some things in which
no amount of temptation will cause
him to waver from what he knows
to be right.
A man knows when and when not to
listen to his friends.
A man is able to prioritize his life.
He knows what is important to him
and his future.
A man has goals and objectives
and strives each day to reach his goals.

23

A man has compassion for his fellow man,
stands up for what he believes in,
does not destroy his family or his friends.
A man puts God first and his family next.
A man can be counted on to
follow through on the things
required of him.
A man takes care of business before pleasure.
With him, obligations are
taken care of before pleasure and pastime.

A man is trustworthy.
A man is kind and gentle.
A man knows that it is not
a woman's duty to clean up behind him.

A man is honest, respectful and dedicated.
A man has character, is warm and loving,
and knows his limits.
A man searches for the truth,
is knowledgeable and thoughtful.
A man is helpful and knows
that his actions build his reputation.
A man does not need alcohol or
drugs to prove his manhood.
A man takes pride in who he is.
A man, my son,
is what I knew, the day you were born,
you would one day become.
A MAN, MY SON, IS YOU.

Walk in Our Steps

My sons, my daughters,
why is it hard for you to walk
in my steps?
Your path would be that much easier for you
as you stride through life.

No, my children, perhaps I've not had the
opportunities you've had,
my education may be limited
to what was allowed me at the time.

You think I do not know anything
and yet, my children, I raised you.
Perhaps there were things
I did not know;
but, I taught you what I knew
at the time.
Then, I gave you an opportunity
to grow and learn.

Because of those who have walked before you,
we blazed a trail for you
and yet our steps
you do not think are safe for you.
You think you must
blaze your own trail.

There may be things in books
that we do not know,
things we've not learned because
the opportunities for knowledge

were not afforded to those of us
who were educated
in the decades of the 60s and before.

You think we do not know
because we struggled so
and yet, we see you
and we know what it is
you think you know
because we have already
been before you where it
is you think you are headed
and we know what is around
the curves, the bends, the crooks
in the road ahead.

We know the disappointments
and we know that the color
of our skin, your skin
will and does make a difference
to those who are not like us.
We know that the dream of
Dr. King is not fulfilled.

Yes, we may sit where we want
on the bus
and eat at most any restaurant
we wish,
but what about the jobs and the housing?
What about our young men
being imprisoned and killing
each other in the streets
over drugs they do not produce?

What of our young people
who are having children
and do not know how to be
a parent?
And yet there's a generation of you
who think we who have trod
the path before you,
do not know.

My children, it is you
who do not know.
It is you who are confused.
Perhaps we did not teach you
to respect yourself as
our grandparents respected themselves.
Perhaps we did not teach you
education was the key to your future.

Well, let us begin now to tell you.
Pull your pants up around your waist
and put a belt on to hold them there.
Tuck you shirt into your waistband.
Stand up straight
with your shoulders squared
and never fear looking
any man in the eye.

Hold your head up,
stop hanging on the street corners,
looking for something to do,
which usually means trouble.
Put down the guns,
leave the gangs,

give the drugs back
to those who encourage you
to take your brother's life.
Get your education,
show respect, and
demand respect in return.

You are worthy,
but you must be prepared for
the journey.
Without a vision you shall perish
and equally so
with the wrong vision, you perish.

As a man thinketh
so is he.
If you see yourself as less than
others
or if you see yourself as nothing,
then that is what you are.
Turn your life around,
start today.
Renounce your past,
begin anew;
it is all up to you.

Yes, we may not have had the
opportunities presented to you,
but we knew how to take
advantage of what was afforded to us
and we know how to survive.

Too Large to Say I'm Sorry

Life brings disappointments,
as we grow and learn.
It is but a twinkling
and then life is gone.
Oft times we do not say
or do the things we can
and never do we realize
until a loved one is gone.
Although we see others die,
somehow we never see
the love that should pass between
we that are free.
We can choose what we do
and how we treat those we are supposed to love.
Yet, we stand by our pride
and let anger stand in our way.
Too large to say, "I'm sorry,"
no apology from me.
You'll never hear the words, "I'm sorry,"
They won't come from me.
Yet, when I sat at a funeral
and it's your body lying before me
then I'll say, "I'm sorry"
and ask you to come back to me.
It's then that my pride is broken
although you can not hear
my heart and soul are weary,
and I apologize to a corpse,
a body that I see.
There is no life, no ear to hear,
no life to answer me.

It's much too late now for us,
too late for you and me;
but what about the ones you've left;
those yet around me.
Why can't we let the past be gone
and begin our life anew,
so when death comes and knocks again
and takes another home,
we will not sit and ache in pain
knowing someone else will never know
we loved them while they were here.

Memories

Yesterday's memories are slowly
    slipping by.
These are the passions shared by
    you and me.
You are the only one
    who knew my passion
        my grief.
You knew my hurt,
    my pain,
the joys that we kept.

You are the only one who's seen
    the tears roll down my cheeks.
Yet, you've gone away and
    left me here to weep.
I love you now,
    as I loved you then.
I cannot release the pain
    that has swelled up within.

And although I remember the
    good times and the bad,
all our dreams we shared
    have shriveled up and died.
Oh, I long for you each night
    by my side
but, that won't happen now
    because you've left me
        and you've died.

HERITAGE

Nat, Harriett, Sojourner, Malcolm and Martin

We, your offspring for whom you suffered and died have failed to
accomplish the freedom for which you strove for us.

We are complacent in our walk and our talk
because we can eat at the "White man's" lunch counter
and sit at the front of his buses,
and yet, our young people are dying in the streets of the ghetto,
created for us as a jungle and we cannot escape.

Moses, where are you my brother?
Weren't you supposed to lead us to the
Promised land?

Where is that land—
that land paved with milk and honey?
Where, for us, are those streets of gold?
Did you bring us to it and let us go
without teaching us how to sustain and
carry it to the next generation and beyond?

Nat, Harriett, Sojourner, Malcolm and Martin
We failed you—
because you died that we might be free,
and yet, we still march and sing
"We shall overcome;"
while our children are being left behind the masses
in educational achievement
and youngsters from lands some of you never imagined
come and claim the gifts you left for us.

The visions you saw for us are not yet
not now; because we have not tried.
We have given up.
We do not teach our children . . .
The civil rights, the justice
for which you fought is not here for us
and yet, we sit by and we reason
that the "White Man" is still keeping us down.

Opportunity has knocked and we've not answered.
Doors have opened and we have shut
them in our wake,
our quest,
our hustle to get over on our own brother
or sister, as it were.

Please Set Me Free

You don't understand my people.
Did you ever really try?
This question from my heart
can only attempt to see
and understand your view;
but I don't have your mind,
nor your experiences;
neither do you share mine.
I can only tell you what I feel.
In the same vain you have
no concept of what I feel
because you've not walked
in my shoes.
You expect me to understand you.
In fact, everything focuses on you.
Me,
I don't matter.
My views are not important
to you,
yet, your views and concepts
are forced on me.

You raped me of my dignity,
you raped me of my heritage—my past.
You took me from my ancestors;
my native land.
You took everything from me;
brought me to a foreign land.
You forced me to forget the land
from which I came.

My language died
somewhere back in my past.
No,
you don't understand my pain
you've not taken the time
to talk with me or to know me
because to you I really do not exist.
I do not matter
for to you I am nothing.

Why take my rage out on my own?
Because my own understand,
although they tend not to condone.
Because I know your laws
are against me.
Your justice,
it's not for me.
It matters not what I do
to myself or my own
as long as I keep my
violence at home.
It does not matter to you
what affects my neighborhood
as long as it does not approach yours.

Why do I riot within my neighborhood,
burn the businesses, and loot the stores?
Because with my own I'm accepted
I'm loved;
when I hurt they hurt.
With my own
my sentence will be just.

If I burned your neighborhood;
I'd be burned at the stake.
If I looted your stores;
I'd be shot as an animal.

Rodney King is but one example
of what I've known
and lived with for centuries.
No, I do not hate you
the person.
I hate your acts, your actions.
But you,
you hate me because to you,
my skin is black.
To you, I'm not worthy.
What will it take for you to see;
to know, that we are
all humans?
The color of one's skin does not matter.
What's inside the soul
is what matters.

I ask you,
Is your soul free?
"And you shall know the truth and
the truth shall set you free."
Let's find the truth,
so that we can all be free.

You don't have to love me;
but I ask that you
do set me free—
free to make my own decisions.

I can not do this with your drugs
controlling me.
Free to live and
work where I choose.
I cannot do this with
you in control of my economic status;
with you forcing me to
be dependent upon you
with your welfare system
and under privileged education.

Why can't you just let me be free?
Free to be the person
God sent me here to be.
When you control all the strings
it's impossible for me
to cut free.
When you hold the scissors
I can't bite the ropes
with my teeth.
Yes, perhaps my violence
is wrong;
but it got your attention.
Now, I ask that you
kindly,
please just set me
F R E E.

Black Man

Black man, Black man,
plant your seed.
Don't let it fall on fallow ground,
take care of it and
watch it grow.
Nurture it as it sprouts,
keep it close to you;
while the roots gather their
strength.
Let your seed know
it can lean on you
to gather that strength.

Black man, Black man,
remove the weeds.
Don't let them
strangle your seed.

Black man, Black man,
stay nearby.
Don't let your seed
wither and die.

Black man, Black man,
who is your seed?
Do you care if
it lives or dies?

Black man, Black man,
tower of strength.
Pass it to the generations
you now breed.

Black man, Black man,
filled with courage.
Don't leave your seed
to be raised by its mother.

Black man, Black man,
there is a need
for you to discipline
your seed.

Shower it with love
that surpasses all other.
Watch it grow into the man
we know our race needs.

Black man, Black man,
raise up your seed
Nurture it,
care for it,
raise it to be
a mighty oak,
like your forefathers.

Freedom

Freedom! Freedom!
Was the cry throughout this land
nearly a century and a half ago
"I is free, you is free—
Now all God's chil'ins is free!"

Tis the cry the slaves proclaimed back in 1863.
They didn't know they were not truly free.

In August 1963, Dr. Martin Luther King, Jr. voiced his *I Have a Dream*
speech standing before the Lincoln Memorial.
"So let freedom ring from the prodigious hilltops of New Hampshire.
Let freedom ring from every hill and molehill of Mississippi
From every mountain side, let freedom ring."
Was his cry.
"And when we allow freedom to ring—black men and white men,
Jews and Gentiles, Catholics and Protestants will be able to join hands
and to sing in the words of the old Negro spiritual,
Free at last free at last; thank God Almighty, we are free at last."
His voice still rings in our ears.

But look at us today, you and me
and I ask you are we yet free?

Oh, there are places we can go and places we can eat;
but have these things made us free?

We may say what we like or will
if politically correct it is.
We might work in places and jobs once forbidden;
and ride buses and street cars sitting right next to
the driver if we will;
but I don't think that's the freedom
we really seek.

To be equal,
that's the key
that is to set each of us free.

When you no longer look at me
and hold my dark brown skin color against me,
when I can one day look at you
and forgive you for what you've done to me.

When we can truly trust each other,
when we judge by character and not by color,
all of us will be set free.

Then and only then can we truly cry clearly
Freedom! Freedom!
Lord, God, Almighty, we are indeed free.

Happy

You all wants me to be happy.
That's what you says to me.
How can I be happy
and I's not free?
You still the boss man;
still looking over me.

I's still a slave
still bound by the master.
No words spoken
yet, master you ain't set me free.

Happy, that word means nothing to me.
Cause you see master
I ain't yet free.

I's ask you how can I be happy
you ain't set me free.
Says you did it
when Mr. Lincoln, President.
Says he set the captive free;
gave some land and said
"Now, you's free."

What I s'pose to do?
How I s'pose to act
when I's free?
Master never 'llowed me
to think afore.
He never set me free.

You still the boss man
you set the pace
and it's you who decides
when I'll be free.

Reflections

Through the mirrors of my mind,
day after day
I see reflections of life itself—
reflections of all the days of old
I can see it as if it were today.
When I was a slave and you
were the boss
yes, I must agree those times
have changed but yet I am not free.
It seems you still have a bond over me.

Through the mirrors of my mind,
as my heart pounds,
I see reflections of life today.
Reflections of what life should be.
Reflections of what it means to me.

RELATIONSHIPS

You Don't Know Me

You don't know me.
Neither I you.
The eyes meet;
there is a smile
not from me for I'm much too shy.

I want to speak,
chat a while;
but, is the smile worth my while
to search you out?

Will you judge me
as the rest?
Have you already put me through a test?

Did I pass?
What is my score?
Dare I speak;
let down my fence.
Have I judged you,
sorted you into a category;
or, is it me I've targeted
fearing I'll not be adequate enough for thee?

I see eyes that sparkle,
a smile,
and yet I don't know that they will really accept me.

Can you speak and make it clear
that from you I have nothing to fear?

I would speak;
but my tongue is tied.
Words won't come from my mouth.
It's all because I am shy.

Or is it that life has taught me
I should not try to be something that I'm not?

That somehow my words won't quiet agree
with those you often speak.
Because my diction is off and my vocabulary is weak.

Strangers when We Met

Strangers when we met and yet
you are part of me and
I am part of you;
but the two of us
will never be more than strangers.

You came into my life
a tall handsome stranger.
You touched a part of me
that no one else can ever see.
You left me without a word
and your voice I'm not
sure I ever heard.

You entered my life
when I was free,
yet you stole a part of me.
Why did I let you touch my life?

Strangers when we met and yet
straight away we knew
that our lives would intertwine
and you would be a part of mine
and I a part of thine.

Strangers when we met and then
oh when we joined hand in hand
your tender touch; a warm embrace,
and an unfamiliar face.
A tender kiss upon my lips—

We're not strangers now.
No, oh no
we're not strangers now.

But way back when
the years gone by has brought us
to this end and
we're not strangers now.

We were strangers when we met and then
you looked into my eyes.
There was something there
my own face became a smile and then
my smile turned into a grin.
A smile perhaps; I'm not sure
or maybe it was the warmth we shared;
a look that fades with the rise
of the morning sun.
Anyway, we're not strangers now.
No, oh no
we're not strangers now.

Our Love Affair

Let me tell you that it's wrong for me.
Yes, I know it's wrong for you.
Why are we doing this?
Meeting in out-of-the way places,
hiding in dark corners of the streets.
We know we don't belong together
you and I;
but, we're having a love affair,
running down back allies
in the middle of the night,
making love together
and letting each other know it was out of sight.
I should be telling my husband,
"Darling I love you more
than there are stars in the sky."
You should be holding your wife;
but instead you and I are cheating on them.
No, actually we are cheating ourselves.
Why don't we just let them go?
Why don't we stop putting on a show?
Are we in love or is it just pretend?
You know baby I really don't know.

All I know is when you hold me close,
when you kiss my lips,
when you hold my hands;
baby, baby, I feel I can understand
you and I having this love affair.
The two of us meeting late at night,
hiding in dark places,
making sure everything is all right.
The two of us, like two kids,
kissing and holding hands,
fighting and making up again.
Life's just too short
let's say good night;
leave our thoughts alone,
start tomorrow anew
just the two of us
in a brand new love affair.

Your Eyes Spoke

The first time I saw you standing
lean,
tall,
strong,
you were silent;
but
your eyes spoke
in a whisper,
which
stroked my very being.

Your lips never parted;
but
your heart said
all the words I longed to hear.
This was the beginning
of a relationship
now parted.
No place to go.
Nowhere to look.
No place to hide
the feelings inside.
Where do we go from here?

We've been lovers;
but
never friends.
What's to happen to you and me?
The walls I built

to shut people out.
You tore down at the
blink of an eye.

I fell in love.
You took flight.
No commitment,
don't dare depend on me.
I can't handle that.
Can't you see?

Yes, you told me this;
but love had blinded me.
The future was not
mine to see.

The night I first saw you
you stood so lean,
so tall,
so strong.
Your eyes smiled
yet your lips did not part.
Your heart spoke to mine
in a whisper;
so gentle,
and when your hand touched mine
there was a spark,
Magic!

A brilliant man
I knew I touched.
What are we to do,
the two of us?
Don't let me go,
for I will drown.
A broken heart,
a wounded mind.
What will you do?
Just as I thought
you cannot leave me;
yet you cannot stay.
Somehow we each
don't know what to say.
It wasn't love
after all,
it was only lust.
And now, we end a relationship
where only two hearts spoke
and we shall never
have this passion for another.
A sad goodbye to
the eyes,
the lips,
the heart,
of the lean,
tall,
strong man,
I beheld across a room
when your eyes spoke.

Wrap Me in Your Strength

I want you to take me in your arms
and love me from evening until dawn.
Embrace me with your maleness.
Wrap me in the folds of your
masculine self.
Engulf me in your care.
I want you to lead me
where I can follow you.
Take me to the edge of life
and back again.

Overwhelm me in your strength.
Let me know you will protect me;
be here for me.
Lead me with your knowledge,
your wisdom,
guide me with your strength.

Reach within the walls of your soul
and secure in me
the stillness, the peace
I see deep within the essence of your very being.
Take me in your arms
and surround me with your love.
Surrender me into your being.
Embrace me with your maleness.
Let me know you are the leader,
the head, the king of my being.

Wrap me in the warmth of you.
Hold me to your truth
that I may never stray from you.
Engulf me in the folds of
arms so long, so lean, so strong.

Stroke me with the tenderness of a heart so warm.
Stand me next to you—
let me help you become all
that you want to be.
Pull me to you with your strength.
Give me hope to see the
future you've prepared
and continue to make
for us
by wrapping me in your strength.

My Lady—My Man

I will respect you because you are my lady.

I will honor you because you are my man.

I'll not be bound by what society or the world
dictates me to be;
but rather by the laws laid out by God.

I will leave mother, father, sister, brother
friend and enemy and I will cleave to you.

I will look to you for strength.
I will hold to the concept of unity.

I will place my trust in you;
hoping and trusting it will never be broken.

We have come to this moment
because we were brought together for a purpose.

Though they are old fashion and outdated
by today's standards—

Let us, as we join together to become one
love, honor and cherish
one another until death.

Let us accept each other as we are
and not attempt to change each other.

For it is who and what we are that brought
the two of us together.

As we go forth from this alter,
let us know that from now through eternity, we are one.

Together we can make it
through any and everything.

Just because you are my lady.
Only because you are my man.
And today we become one.

Do Not Leave Me

Do not leave me to think about what you have meant to me.
Do not leave me to mourn you once you're gone.
Do not leave me here alone.

I will not survive the pain caused
by your absence from me.
I'll not survive the misery of the hour;
the day you leave me
to think about the years I've given myself to you.

Do not leave me for another.
Do not go away from me.
Do not let go of what we've shared.

I'll not survive the loneliness.
I'll not survive your departure.
I'll not survive without you by my side.

Take me with you when you go.
Take me to that other shore.
I'll not make it here alone.
I'll not make it with you gone.

I can't stand the pain of you leaving.
I can't make it any other way.
I've loved you for so long now.
I'll not make it with you gone.

Do not leave me to myself.
Do not leave me to think of you alone.
Do not leave me here to stay
without you for even one day.

I'll not make it without you.
I'll not survive your absence.
I'll not survive the loss.

The Redwoods Bring Memories

Looking at the Redwood trees
bringing back the memories of yesteryears.
It's too bad you had to go,
had to leave.
I just hope that one day soon
you'll be home
'cause looking at the Redwood trees
brings back so many memories.

Memories that I can't stand too long.
Oh, please come home.
Please write and let me know
when you'll be home.
I don't know just what to do
with you gone.
But looking at these Redwood Trees
is not enough.

Sometimes I sit and think of you
till dusk.
And then when the sun is gone away,
I cry and laugh at the same time.
Cry because you're not here,
laugh at the things we once did;
but looking at the Redwood trees
brings back the memories of yesteryears.

Today I got a letter in the mail.
It was from his mom and it read,
"Sorry you have to hear this way
the sad news just came today of his death.
I know he meant a lot to you
as did he to us.
So keep looking at the Redwood trees
and let them hold the memories of yesteryears.

Please don't let this get you down
keep on going dear
for he would not like for you to cry;"
but, I cry anyway,
I can't help but loving him this way.
And I keep looking at the Redwood trees,
letting them bring the
happy memories.

Because I Thought You Were My Friend

Over the years that we have known each other,
we have shared many things.
We have been through tough times
through times of pain and times of joy.

We have sat with one another through miscarriages
and broken hearts.
We have shared the ups and downs of marriage
and the trials of having and not having children.

We have shared the heartaches family can
sometimes cause us to endure.
We have shared tears of joy and tears of sadness;
but through it all we remained friends.

Lately I have felt that you have needed me much
more than I need you.
I have tried to be there for you;
but the years are creeping up on the two of us
and we are settling into our own.

I know we have both made mistakes;
but how often do I call attention to the
ones you've made?
Yet, you choose, at every chance
to call attention to all of mine.
Some are as old as the years we've known each other;
others are conjured in your mind.

Yes, we have dealt with many things:
boyfriends, husbands, and lovers.
children, nephews and nieces
mothers, fathers, sister and brothers
even aunts and uncles.

Because I thought you were my friend
I have shared so many, many things with you.
Some of which I wanted to die with the wounds
that tore my heart apart.
But for some reason, unknown to me,
you refuse to allow the past to die.

Why do you keep the hurt and pain
so close at hand each day?
Why do you call upon the past
so many others have put away?

It is sadness that I see in the eyes
of a woman who use to be my friend.
It causes me such pain and grief
to know that she now faces such misery.

How dare you want me to share
in the world
you created for yourself.
I choose not to linger in the past;
but try to grow each day.
I try to love and not to hate.

I try my best not to judge
and let my wounds slowly heal.
I try to let the sadness die
or rest outside my door.
But you, the person I thought a friend
keep bringing the burdens in.

Why do you wish to weigh me down
with such heartache and pain?
What is it that I have not or
that you wish to gain?
My life has held so much to bear
and I've shared it with my God.
Why can't you leave me at my rest
and let me befriend you now?

Because I thought you were my friend
I let you enter in
and all I can see within my life
is how you try to destroy me.

I Dare Not

Because you mean so much to me
and because I care;
I dare not break your silence;
I dare not interfere.

Although I long to hear from you,
it seems that you do not care.
I make the best with what I have;
a treasured thought,
a memory of the past.
When you needed me
I was there.

Now that I want to hear from you
time passes on;
I hear nothing.
If I try to contact you,
you are busy and can't be disturbed.

What would it take for you to speak,
just a little 'hi'?
And then you could return to your schedule
and I would have something
I could use for perhaps
a lifetime—

But when I call or come by
and you won't answer me,
it's then I think, but why?

Wasn't I there when you needed me?
Can't the favor be returned?
But you're much too busy for me now;
you have a brand new life.
Well guess what.
so do I.

I just happen to treasure family
and friends
and hold them dear to me.
Perhaps that is why I can say
you are busy,
although I know it's a lie.

You have time for others,
yet you say I should not cry.
Well, when you will not answer my calls
and hide behind the door,
then I guess tis I that have won and you've
lost your friend in me.

Am I Missing You, You Say

Am I missing you? You say.
Am I missing you? You say.
Am I missing you? You say.

I checked my phone
every minute
of every day
that you were away.
Am I missing you? You say.

I have cried myself
to sleep each night
since you went away.
Am I missing you? You say.

In the middle of
the night,
I hold my pillow tight,
thinking only about you.
Am I missing you? You say.

Am I missing you? You say.
I want to say, "I'm not
missing you at all;"
but that would be a lie
'cause every minute,
every second,
every hour of every day
I think of what
might have been.
Am I missing you? You say.

Am I missing you? You say.
Am I missing you? You say.
Am I missing you? You say.

(This is more a song than a poem)

We Are One

We were two when we met;
now we are one and not tired yet.

Relationships are supposed
to be this way.

You met me,
I met you.
Now it's we.

The two of us are one
and no one can tear us apart.

Relationships like ours are based on
love and hope—
the future.

Together, we will last and
forever we will be as one.

You and I are all we have
and that's enough to withstand
the Universe . . .

because
we have indeed become
ONE.

Understand

I love you and I do wish you would stay;
> but
if you choose to go, I'll not stand in the way.
Go ahead, make the move
> that you feel you must.
I'll not cry for the loss.
"Why?"
> You say, if I care.
Because in life when one cares,
> they must realize that in order to
allow growth
> there must be a letting go.
And though I know you think
> that this is best,
I'll not be the one
> who puts it to the test.
Go forth in your youth
> conquer what you must.
As age and wisdom takes your hand,
> remember back and know
I was the one you could trust the most.
Although it saddens me to see you leave,
> this I understand.
Though you say that it is me you
> really can't work beside,
> > I understand.
And though you feel that life dealt with you unfairly,
> this I understand;
but do you understand
> the things life has dealt to me?

I Love You, Good-Bye

I love you darling
but I feel I must say "Good-bye"
and I sit down and cry.

It seems like only yesterday that we met
and when you said those magic words, I wept.

Then after being engaged for two whole years,
we were wed.

And after the honeymoon,
which lasted three years, came the tears.
When I discovered a babe was on the way,
it brought the fears.

Looking back on those years,
I quickly go to tears.

Now I feel my life with you
is about to end.
That is why I say right now
"Darling, I love you;
But, I feel I must say, "Good-bye".

If only you would let me grow,
not have me sit home both night and day.

I have the feeling I don't belong
and I must see if I can make it on my own.

You say you won't know what to do
with me gone.
I'd like to see you try
to make it on your own.
That may be the reason I'm leaving you all alone.
I know that you feel it makes no sense
for me to live away from you.

You've always provided me with the
basic necessities you felt I needed;
but somehow it's not enough.
Thus I have run away;
I need some time;
I need some space to be by myself,
alone.
I no longer wish to be a housewife
sitting home day and night.

Somehow it seems with my work all done,
I find myself just staring into space.
What would happen should you leave or die?
I'd be lost, nowhere to turn.

I would not know what steps to take;
which roads to choose for fear of mistakes.

That is why I'm saying it now
for tomorrow may be too late.
I love you darling;
but I really must get away.

All I ask is that you just give me time to grow,
I'm not sure if I can stay away.

I want to make it on my own
while I still have hope.

Please try to understand
what it is I'm saying
and perhaps one day soon I'll return to you.

But as for now my sweet love
I think of our lives and I cry.
Deep inside I feel that
I have died.

Always remember this
as my parting words to you,
"I love you darling, but I must say
good-bye"

Pressed Between the Pages of My Mind

Memories, pressed between the pages of my mind
when they're lost are so very hard to find.
Memories are what you have to hold to
when your loved one is gone away.

So always remember the good times that you had,
forget all the bad times
because they hurt so bad.
When you look back on those sweet memories,
you'll find peace of mind,
happy times from all those memories.
Just don't let the sad ones get you down.

Memories, pressed between the pages of our minds.
Memories, when they're lost, will never ever be found.
Memories, looking through the pages of my mind,
memories, sweet memories of our past.
You were young and so was I
when we built those memories to last.

Memories, pressed between the pages of my mind.
Memories, that are often hard to find.
How could you forget such sweet memories?
The memories of our life—
memories that touch my mind
like wine touches my lips.

Those are the years I dare not forget;
looking back over the pages of my mind;
searching for the precious memories
of our yesterdays.
Though I look through the pages,
I can't seem to find what caused
us to breakup this last time.
Those memories are not pressed
between the pages of my mind.

You Are Married

You asked me this question once before,
I felt that I could not let you know.
But once again you ask of me
what the future holds for the two of us
and all that I can see is
that you are married
and me;
I am free.

You have no right to choose
and I won't be a fool.
Why is it so hard for me?
Life is not easy;
I know;
but why are you tempting me?
Knowing the two of us
can never be as one
because you are married
and me,
I am free.

No Communication

Gone she was for close to a year,
six months some say,
eight say others.
I don't know, I'm just her Admin support.

No one said to me,
       especially her;
she never communicated with her staff;
other than to say
       what was done wrong;
or, criticize something not performed.

She's back now,
       no "Good morning",
just as there was no "Good bye".

Just showed up.
       Just as she disappeared.
When she left,
       vanished
       with no trace.
Arrived
       with no announcement.

Is this in order to catch someone at their worst?
Or yet,
asleep.
Keep a watchful eye on her.
Because she is certainly looking at you
in hopes of finding a way,
a means of letting you go.

No, don't expect to hear a thing
from her.
She won't communicate
unless it is to let one know
things done wrong
or not done at all,
unless
of course she is saying good bye
to you
because she has found a way
to rid herself of your
presence by letting you go.
No communication,
just cut
and
you're gone.

INSPIRATIONS

What is Christmas?

I know what Christmas is about.
Do you?
It is not about bells that jingle
nor a red nosed reindeer.
Christmas is not about the
toys and things that
a child chance to find under a tree.
It's not about a man
of snow
or someone naming him
Frosty you know.
Christmas is not about the carols we sing
nor the feast for which our parents spring.
Christmas is really about
the birth of a babe
born many years ago
in the town of Bethlehem.
Christmas is about the songs the angels sang
and the star that guided the wise men by night.
Christmas is about the gifts they brought
when they were welcomed at the site.

Christmas is about the joys
brought to the heart of man
that he could be born again.
Christmas is about the Virgin birth
of a young girl, Mary.
Christmas is about a belief we have
that Christ had no earthly father.
Christmas, yes I know
just what it is all about
and it's not about the bows and ribbons
or boxes and gifts.
Christmas is not about what one gives or gets.
The true meaning of Christmas
is that God gives us the miracle of life
that we might be blessed.

What Shall I Do?

There are times in life
when you just don't know what to do.

Family all grown up
and your spouse has died,
children all moved away.
Friends are very few
and when you go to them,
they don't have time for you.
That's when you may ask
"Lord, what shall I do?"
and you wait for an answer
but it seems somehow not to get through to you.
Can't go to your friends;
they all depend on you.

So you try again to ask
"Lord, what shall I do?"

Though you tarry there
and say you have not a care,
it seems that once again
no words come,
no voice is heard,
no words come back to you.
What is there to do now?
Who can you turn to?
"Lord, I'm leaving it all up to you.
Please, please Lord
tell me what to do.
I'll ask you again and again
until you get through to me.
Dear, dear Lord
tell me just what I should do."

Goodbye Old Year Hello New

Goodbye to the old year.
Hello to the new.
We gladly welcome you.

As the days turn,
like the pages of a book,
keep me in good health.

As the nights grow old
and the morning cold,
teach me to love life more.

Goodbye old year.
Hello new.
Give honor to those
to whom it is due.

Goodbye old year.
Take with you
my weary thoughts.

Hello to the new.
Bring me more
pleasant thoughts with you.

Give peace to those who
long for it in you.

Bring happiness to the hearts
of all who see you come this way.

Goodbye old year.
Take with you the hate and pain,
you've caused all the year through.

Hello to the New Year.
As you come shinning through
bring with you love
to last the whole year through.

What Was in that Cup?

"What was in that cup?"
I heard the preacher say
one Palm Sunday morn
What was in that vile and bitter cup;
that caused my Master to pray
"Lord, if it be Thy will
remove this cup from me?"
(When my Savior prayed
in the Garden of Gasemene)

What was in the cup?
The future for you and me.
What was it my Master saw
and did not wish to be?
Was it the suffering and
loss of souls like yours or mine?
What was in the cup that day
that vile and bitter cup
that caused my Master to
almost give up on you and me?
Did he see the hate and pain
mankind cause today?
Did he see before His eyes
the laden despair?

Did He see the rapes and muggings
and a world full of sin?
Is this the something in the cup
my Master took within?
Is that why He did not speak
that day on Calvary?
Because of the bitterness in that cup
He held in the garden of Gasemene.

What was in that cup
from which the Lord did drink?
A wretched world yet to come
of which the prophets told.
What was in the cup
besides His death as was told,
His rising from the grave,
His children to proclaim.
What was in the cup
besides the Lord's own blood
that He shed for you and me?

No Room

They sought a room for to lay the babe,
but the innkeeper said,
No room in this Inn.

No where to go
and a babe to be born;
they sought a room
and again were told,
No room in the Inn

No where to go,
no where to turn.
A babe is waiting for to come
it won't be long,
for he's on his way.

Where shall they go?
Where shall she lie?

Only a stall in a stable.
Only a stall in a stable, here.

Mary gave birth to her first-born child
and laid him in the manger—
a bed of straw was all she had
for to lay her babe
because everyone had said
There is no room;
no room in the Inn.

Laid in a Manger

Many years ago in a stable cold
a babe was born to a virgin girl.
She wrapped him in swallowing clothes
and in a manger laid him.

Poor little Jesus born on Christmas Morning
in the town of Bethlehem
far, far away.
Wise Men came to worship him,
and brought him
Gold, Frankincense, and Myrrh.

Upon his birth, a star shorn bright
and stood above the stable.
Shepherds left their flocks that night
and followed a star low and bright.

Poor little Jesus child, born of a virgin
in the town of Bethlehem
that first Christmas morning.

Wise Men sought to worship him,
Kings sought to kill him,
and angels sang above
Glory to God in the highest
for Jesus Christ is born this day
in the town of Bethlehem
far, far away.

If I should have been there
on that one night
what would I have given him?

Should I have been a shepherd,
would I have left my flock
and followed the star that shorn so bright?
Had I been a rich man,
would I have adorned him with riches?
Or would I have sought him
as a king with jealous rage?

A babe, a babe in a stable born,
laid in a manger filled with hay
that first Christmas Day.

SOCIETY/SOCIAL CONCERNS

You've Taken All of Me

You've taken my mind
and now you want
my soul.
Is there anything of me
you care not to hold?

As long as you
can keep me
this way,
you will feel superior.

But now that I have grown,
you're afraid,
threatened that
I will get away.

If I should but learn to speak as you,
you are afraid
you will no longer hold a bond
over me.

You don't want me to leave
for without me,
you are lost and alone.

But you must realize that
I have needs just as you
and perhaps
someday the two of us
can meet in harmony.

Why don't you give up the hate
you hold for me?
Because despite
the things you have done
to me,
I don't hate you.

I hate myself for allowing
you to do these things to me.
I cannot understand
why you treat me
as you do.
It must be
that you hate yourself
more than you hate me
and in order to
make yourself feel better
you take your misery out on me.

If the two of us could
grow together,
it would come to a
pleasant peace
and neither of us would have to be
in this needless misery.

What can now come of us?
Should we not turn away
from the hate that we have
held so long?
Our enemy in the course of time
will come as a thief in the night
and destroy the two of us.
By this
what will either of us
have gained?

You need me and I need you.
So why not admit this
and from it grow?
Is it too much to ask
that we might conquer our past
and in this be able to make
a more pleasant future?

Can the whole world look at us and see
what is so obvious to be?
And yet the two of us
are blinded by the things that used to be.

Let us now awaken and see
the light that before us be
and end the strife and battle;
meet in
peace and harmony.

You took my culture; my goals
you took my music; my voice
even my acting and left me no choice.
You took my homeland
yet won't share yours.
Perhaps it's because you are scared.
You've taken everything from me;
is there anyone who really cares?
All that I ask of you now is that we
share peace, show love and live
in harmony.

Twenty-Two is a Good Age

Twenty-two is a good age, you know
and yet, one has many a years to grow.

I remember being that age
a decade or so ago
and
twenty-two is a nice age, you know.

It's a time to remember,
a time to learn,
a time to grow,
time to look back at the years gone by;
time to plan for those years ahead
and
twenty-two is a nice age, you know.

Life at this age is a good one
for one is somewhat totally free.

You can get up with the dawn;
or chase the sun to the sea—
no responsibilities,
only lots of fun.

It's a time to look forward to growing older and wiser.
A time to reflect on yesterday's joys,
which had no real sorrow.

Twenty-two is a good age
. . . you know!

Nine-Eleven

Across the Eastern skies
they came.
Flying American and United
wings.

Foreign students
upon our soil
they learned to fly our planes.
It was for freedom they proclaimed
they came.

Twin Towers standing high,
beautifully displayed against the sky.
Languages of the world,
inside the ones that stood
side by side,
yielding eleven.

Marking the gateway
to a new day—
a new beginning;
a freedom unknown
to those who should come.

New York City
the Towers stood;
so vast and strong.
Showing unity to the world as
they rested in the quietness of the dawn.

Who knew the evil lurking in the mist
of the September morn?
Nine-eleven
emergency—emergency
the echoes of the calls,
cell phones;
loved ones called.

Calls can't get through;
blocked by something in the airways,
echoed as the silence
shattered beneath the open sky.

Towers standing side by side,
collapsed and fell to the ground.

In the predawn hours,
of 9/11
evil lurked beyond our shores;
it was not a moment's thought
that brought them
forth from the night.
They said they answered freedom's call
as they tumbled our walls.

The Twin Towers,
side by side they stood
as the planes came
striking them down
to the ground.

Cries of the Young

A young girl dies,
the community cries,
yet no one hears.

Violence is a part of our society
the screams of society
are not in favor of the dead,
they go instead to the heads.

Who really cares that a young life is taken?
Not the society of the shallow.

Gangs are here to place fear.
People, oh people can you hear
the cries that echoes in the street?

Saying, "Isn't it time
for us to beat the hate and
violence of our past?"

Can't we see it will not last?
Mothers are younger year by year.
Oh society, will you hear?

Fathers give up their seed,
never knowing what child they breed.
Society says not to fear.

We will care for the lad;
but later on, hands a gun
to the child not long born—

not mature enough to hold their own;
making choices of false response.

Had I By Chance

We go inside and close our doors;
not just from the bitter cold.
We won't look out the window;
we're much too scared.

Another child, a lad
lies in the dirt;
on the pavement of the sidewalk,
where the street sweeps
dare not sweep.

Blood flows;
veins make the body cold.
Another body;
another life to never grow old.

Young men dying,
no past, no future,
stories never told of how
they died.

Lifeless bodies in the street
and we Christians
do not seek a way
to keep the children out
of the streets.

He's not my child.
I can sleep,
afraid though
I am to cross the street
to speak to him during his life.

Perhaps I could have
prevented his dying,
had I by chance
stopped to speak.

Change

Lifestyles change,
names often stay the same.

People play a lot of games.
"What?" do you say.

We just stay the same,
looking back over the years of time.

Oh, how the people of the world have changed,
searching to find a lifelong dream.

If they could just remain the same,
why do we have to change?

Everyday the styles of life change.
Someone somewhere changes a name;

but the two of us
shall always remain the same.

Life can go on running its eternal game;
but the two of us—
let us remain the same.

Silent Lips

Lips have fallen silent
never to part again.
Why bother to speak
where there are no ears
that hear?

For the heart that cries,
yes, the silent lips
they hear
and too they know.
They have seen
with sad eyes of sorrow—
the injustices;
they have felt the pain
they have toiled the land.

Yes, these silent lips
once had a goal,
a common plan
known to all men,
yet the lips are silent;
as silent as a night
with only the moon and stars.

They know of the anger
that swells up within their race;
they know of the battle that is
forever lost.

Why should I speak when
there are no ears
that hear me?
Why should I waste my breath?

Yes the lips remain silent.
Silent because they have read the history
of a people, lost.
Silent because no one
else seems to care.
Silent because there are no ears
that listen.
Silent for there are no hearts
that care.

The eyes of these lips
keep seeing.
The eyes,
they see the wrong;
but the ears of those around
refuse to listen.
Those ears just refuse to hear.

Should the eyes
then be blinded?
Should they turn the head aside,
and let the lips
keep silent to the ears
that refuse to hear?

Man Leave Me Be

Man, you best to gone now
I done told you once;
it's best that you gone
and leave me 'lone
for man I's done told you once.

Best you gone now,
best you leave me be.
Been married to you now
near half a century
and I's tired of you botherin me.

I's done raised up them youngens of your'n,
fifteen or so we had.
Now that I's sixty-five
I's takin back my pride.

Don't need no more chillens in my life
I's tired now, man—
tired of you botherin me.

So like I says befoe,
it's best you gone now,
best you leave me be.

Was Home So Bad?

Was home so bad we had to leave the past?
The memories made,
the deeds done,
the friendships that were born.

Were we so wrapped in another world,
we'd forsake our own?
What about those years growing up,
the days of our youth?
Was life so bad we must not recall the days,
the weeks, the years?

What about the mentorship; the wisdom of the aged,
did they not teach us to be proud of who or what we are?
What about the love for brother or of just another?

How does one forget and not regret a home
lost and forgotten?
How can we forget the struggle of our parents
(our mothers and our fathers)?

We've let go, the struggle and left behind
our brothers, sisters, cousins.
Guns, drugs and violence
now call them home above.

Was home so bad we had to leave it for another
a world where we're not accepted
just because of color,
a world in which we will forever struggle?

Was home so bad we do not know
that we have to stay to fix it?

It's Not Time For Me

It's not yet time for me to see the things I see;
but yet I see.
'tis not time for me to hear the things my
ears sometime endure;
but yet I hear.

Although I should not say all the things I say,
sometimes I speak them anyway.
It's all because I've grown up too soon;
become wise beyond my years,
and I know just what it is
to experience pain and tears.

As I look into the years ahead,
I find that I have a lot of fears.
And I know the world
feels that I should;
but it's not helping me to cope
with the things I was never taught.

Sometimes I should forget about
the things I see
and should not see;
the things I hear that I should not hear
and often time I should not let
the words come from my mouth
that I should not say.

I just found this out from a friend
and now my life can begin.

No Man Heard My Cry

I called out for help.
No man heard my cry.

Now dear Lord I turn to you,
There's just you and I.

I cannot begin to tell you
of the suffering that I've done.

I know within my heart,
you know my story well.

You have brought me through the storm;
you've brought me through the rain.

Yet I do not know
in you there's no blame.

You see dear Master up above,
man has taught me well.

When things don't go as I think they should,
I'm to find someone to blame

and in my deep despair,
I turned my anger on you,

for Lord, it was you who brought me here.
Why shouldn't you be to blame?

I look back now on my youth,
dark days yet to come.

I remember what mother said back in
those days, long past.

"There is no fault in Jesus, child.
The fault lies with man."

Then I begin to pray again,
"Lord take me as I am;

for I'm just a tiny lamb
about to go astray;
but Lord, if You will mold me now;
in Your hands I'll stay.

Take me, Lord and use me
as You may wish

and let me forever know
blame lies not with You."

SELF-ESTEEM

Individual Unique Me and You

I am a unique individual
and because of it,
no one can ever be me.

No one else can think or do
the things that I think and do
exactly as I think and do
because no one else is me.

I am indeed one unique
individual
and no one else
can ever be
ME.

You are a unique individual
and because of it,
no one will ever be exactly like you.

No one will ever do or think
things as you think and do them;
therefore no one else is you.

You are indeed one unique individual
and no one else
will ever be
YOU.

It's Hard to Know

It's hard to know how to step to you
when for years we've been estranged.

It's hard to know the words to say
when in grief, you're lain.

It's hard to know how to hold your hand
or hold you close in an embrace or hug
when the years gone by have kept us at
a distance.

It's hard to know when to let you know
that I have feelings too
and there are times I wanted to
tell you just how much I cared.
But time and distance has kept us
separated.

It's hard to know how to break the chains
that have bound us to a past,
long gone,
and thrust us into a future that will
not allow us to be
because of the blindness a society
has forced us to accept,
for our classes were cast the day
we were conceived.

Perfect

I am not as anyone else; yet I am perfect
because it is God who has made me
and you see,
He never intended for me to be like you
or you to be like me.
That is why He made each of us
the way in which we could be
one perfect, original individual.

You Don't Scare Me

You don't scare me,
no sir.
Ain't nothing more
than a bully, anyhow.
You may have scared others,
be they friend or foe.
They backed away
and they'd run and hide;
But, "Mister Bully"
You don't scare me,
because I know a secret
on you, anyhow.

RANDOM THOUGHTS

Memories of Yesteryears

Memories of the past keep staring me in the face,
as I look out the window at the trees.

Why should the memories of the yesteryears
haunt me now?

Is there any wonder why I stay awake at night and cry?
Memories of the past will not pass me by.

The ghost of tomorrow sees me now—
memories of yesterday and only in a special way

can make me happy about our last days.
It seems to be a shame for me to think of you

and cry this way;
but who is left to blame?

There was only you and I.
No one else could possibly know how we felt;

but looking out the window now,
staring at the bright blue sky

and asking myself what is left of you and I.
Could you please come back to me?

This time I will let you stay.
Never will I ask you to go away.

Memories of the past are haunting my heart.
Is there something I can do to make this feeling pass?

Memories of the yesteryears are forever
holding onto my soul.

Memories that frighten me still,
yet I'm not willing to let the past be over.

No, I'm not willing to let it go.

Dawn a New Day

As the sun creeps over the mountain tops
and casts the dew aside,
the dawn of a new day arrives
and we see vast new skies.
There is a new life added;
another baby born;
but as the day turns into dusk
another eye closes
with the sunset over the tide.
We go beyond to catch a glimpse of what life may bring
and we find that life offers us many things.

Thoughts

Thoughts, they come and go as a ship in the night.
They glimpse the past
linger on what is now, and blink into the future
What was—is—and shall be.

Thoughts, sometimes of a reality
perceived of a truth;
but what is your truth
may not be the truth of others,
for your perception is not
the same as that of another.

Thoughts, linger in the outer edges of a mind,
into the subconscious of a soul;
waiting, wanting, needing to be released
into a world searching for peace.

Death

Death, the ultimate silencer
causes life to cease,
thoughts are no more.
In death we cannot speak,
see, hear, or feel.

The end of what we know.
Cares are gone.
We no longer worry.

Death, eternal sleep—
life we no longer seek.
Rest in peace—
a breath—
we no longer take.

Silent, in the grave we lie;
never knowing who may pass us by.
Silent tears no longer fall
down cheeks once so warm.

Silent whispers fall
on ears yet sleeping in silence, still.
Heart beats no longer throb
to raise a chest or release a breath.

The soul is gone beyond the grave
and death has ended the life
once full of spirit,
death has taken us to eternal sleep.

What Has Become of the Men of Our Ages?

What has become of the men of our ages?
Have they faded with the time
or have they all gone crazy and
simply lost control of their minds?

I remember yesterday and how we
shared each moment of the day.
Somehow today I feel that I've lost you
in the maze.
You don't show me your feelings;
you sit and stare at the ceiling.

What has become of the boys of yesterday?
They are men now and they have gone astray.
Did you know that I still love you?
Are you wondering why I'm still around?
Is it hard for you to express your love for me?

Do you think that I'm too shy?
Is there a reason for the silence?
Have I done something wrong?
Then, why the heavy sighing;
is it because your love is gone?

What has become of the men of our ages?
Have they faded with the times?
Used to be you'd say you loved me,
used to be you'd greet me with a smile.
Now I can walk with you in silence
and you never open you mouth.
How I miss the things we once shared,
the happiness of the hour.
How I miss your tender kisses.

What has become of the men of our ages?
They have faded with the times.

Just a Simpleton

I'm just a simpleton
born to the commoners of this land.
I like to sit and stare
at the things nature brings me.

Yesterday, I watched a squirrel
feeding on a nut in an acorn tree.
This was of great pleasure to me.

I'm just a simpleton
born to the commoners of this land.
I like to look at the things
the earth holds in bound for me.

I often sit at my window and
watch the ships pass along the bay.
I like to watch the waves of
the ocean as the sun sets in the sky.

Most of all, I like to take a moment to
thank God for the wonders that He has
shared with the commoners of His earth.

For I'm just a simpleton
born to the commoners of this land.

Sympathy

What is sympathy?
A heart felt pain of grief
expressed in time of sorrow,
when joy of yesterday escapes us for a day
because one we loved
has somehow slipped away.

Sympathy is the pain we feel because
words cannot express what we feel.

Sympathy is the anger because we cannot control
or bring our loved ones back to life.

Sympathy is what we feel of death
because we cannot examine
or explain its depths.

Sympathy is knowing that we must trudge on;
that we must somehow face tomorrow.
Sympathy is pain and grief and death.

Yesterday

Yesterday is only
24 hours gone by.
Today brings me closer
to the steps of death.
Does anyone know the heartache
tomorrow will bring?
Does anyone know the pain?

Yesterday has gone and passed me by.
I think of tomorrow and sit down and cry.
Today has just begun for the two of us.
How long will it last?

Yesterday is a thing of the past.
Today, there's hope that
our love will last.

Tomorrow is just another wish away;
but not all wishes come true.

Yesterday, you left behind
your sad and distant past.
Today, you're building on
dreams that will last.
When will you stop
dwelling on the past?

Yesterday is gone now,
never to return.
Today is here.
Let's make of it some good.
Let's not think about tomorrow
for it's not promised to us anyway.

If I Give Myself

If I should but give myself to thee,
will thou love me at the break of day
or once thou lustful passion's filled
will thou leave me for another still?

Just An Ordinary Day

As I awaken with the dawn,
get out of bed with the sun,
and begin a fresh new day;

it's into the bathroom;
wash my hands and face,
into the kitchen start breakfast on its way
get the kids up,
feed the pets
put breakfast on the table—
back to the bathroom;
take a shower, comb my hair and fix my face.

Then it's off on the run
to the schools and the sitters
on the freeway to my job.

Is there any wonder why I'm tired?
Get to work a quarter of seven
start the coffee, take dictation
sit down; begin to type.

The boss wants to see you
and the meeting is beginning late.
Into his office; shut the door,
just a little something I want to let you know.

Back outside; answer the phone
wondering if I'm needed anymore.
Time for lunch
run out the door,
got some shopping, no time to loaf.

Half pass twelve, got to go.
Only a few more hours to go.
Back to work; rings the phone
"Hon, could you please stop by
and drive me home?"
Now, the boss comes through the door.
"Well, Hon, bye, got to run.
Yes, I'll pick you up and drive you home."

"Yes, sir, Mr. So-and-so.
You say you want to dictate;
but do you realize that it's late?"

I Heard An Owl Call My Name

Walking through the forest,
all alone one night,
through the dark and quietness;
my eyes searched for light.

As I walked, I tried to sing;
but words caught in my throat
and I began to choke.
It was quiet and spooky.
My heart began to race
and as I started out to run,
I heard a voice call out my name.

I stopped right in my tracks.
I whirled around to look;
but nothing could I see.
"It must be my nerves," I said,
as I quickened my steps;
but then an owl flew right by me
and flapped its wings near my ears.
"Go away you bird!
Shoo!", I said.
But it paid me no mind.
As the quietness settled down;
I heard my name again.
"Who is that calling me?
Where are you?", I said.
"Come on out and show yourself!"

But the only thing I could see
was an owl coming towards me
and as he came, I could see
that it was he
who was calling me.

I heard an owl call my name.

No One Never Cared About Me

Since you don't care about me now,
please, don't grieve my body when I die.
For just like Tina Turner said
"When I die, dig no hole for my grave
just cremate my body and throw the ashes in the sea
nobody never cared about me."

I know what you say;
but baby, I also see what you do
and to me, words speak low, very low;
but now honey actions I can read loud and clear.

Believe me when I say that sometimes it's hard to
smile and not frown;
especially when I see you fooling around.
Then, you come home late at night
and want me to believe that homemade lie.

Why can't you try to see what life means to me?
Although I know that you really don't care,
I must go on and live
someday I know I'll be free.

As life brings me a brand new day,
I look to the sky and see what is ahead
and although you never really cared about me,
it doesn't matter now.

Just remember this one little thing for me
and when I die, please don't try to grieve over me.
Just cremate my body and dump the ashes in the sea
because I know you never really cared about me.

It's not your fault.
I want you to know and hear it from me,
no one else has ever cared for me.
That's why I ask that no one cry over me.

If I should die, pleased don't dig a grave.
Just burn my body and throw the ashes into the sea—
no one never cared for me.

Fathers Are

Fathers are husbands and brothers and lovers,
sometimes they are friends who keep you from trouble.
Fathers are daddies and uncles and cousins, and such.
Fathers are people you laugh with and quarrel with;
they are the ones you sometimes might fight with;
but fathers are also the ones who brings you joy.

Laughter is Not For Me

Laughter is not for me.
No, not I.
Somehow I just don't
have the tears to cry.
Perhaps, the fears along the years
have dried the tears from my eyes.
Tis sad to say;
but much so true,
I yet have no reason for to die.
For if I die, you see
no one would cry after me.
I would be alone to brood
about the sorrows of this life.

Laughter, on my face?
No, not even a grin
can I bring.
For life has me in oft much pain
and for to die,
what shall I gain?
No heartache and no pain,
at least for the ones I leave behind,
there'd be rejoicing that I were gone.
Not a tear shed to ease their pain
and as the years pass on
and these grow old,
they too would have no laughing
for to bring.
Life will also have caused them pain,
so, as I sit in this mist,
I find the joys life also brings
Yet, no laughter does it bring for me.

Doubt

What could have been
is not
because there was doubt,
erased what was,
caused a new beginning—
A negative disposition.
But was it doubt
or was this the end of things
begun back at the beginning—
A world not known today,
destiny came
and went.
Was it by choice or
doubt that we became who we are?
If reality is believing in the positive,
why do things go wrong
for those who believe in winning
the lottery?
Does doubt seep into a
crevice of the mind,
to unwind the need
to succeed?

A new life we lead—
Choice!
Doubt?
What causes the decay,
the corrosion that eats away at who we are?
Making our yesterdays
a wasteland of
self-hate,
moving into a tomorrow—
A quest for what we wanted today
that ceased because
our choice was doubt.

01/15/2012 Lite Rail Station at 16th Street, Sacramento, CA

Today, Tomorrow, Yesterday

Today is that tomorrow I promised you yesterday,
would come your way tomorrow
and that brought about today
and now again, today, I promise your tomorrow,
which will make yesterday of today.